ED EMBERLEY'S DRAWING BOOK

 OF ANIMALS

LITTLE, BROWN AND COMPANY
BOSTON · TORONTO

OTHER BOOKS
BY ED EMBERLEY:
THE WING ON A FLEA
THE PARADE BOOK
COCK A DOODLE DOO
ROSEBUD
PUNCH AND JUDY
LONDON BRIDGE IS FALLING DOWN
GREEN SAYS GO

IF YOU LIKE THIS BOOK YOU WILL ALSO LIKE:
"ED EMBERLEY'S DRAWING BOOK, MAKE A WORLD"

LIBRARY OF CONGRESS CATALOG CARD NO. 75-107232
NINTH PRINTING
PUBLISHED SIMULTANEOUSLY IN CANADA BY LITTLE, BROWN AND COMPANY (CANADA) LTD.
PRINTED IN THE UNITED STATES OF AMERICA
TR 00672 25 S2
LB 04763 34 I2

FOR THE BOY I WAS,
THE BOOK I COULD NOT FIND

IF YOU CAN DRAW THESE SHAPES, LETTERS, NUMBERS AND THINGS→

YOU WILL BE ABLE TO DRAW ALL THE ANIMALS IN THIS BOOK.

FOR INSTANCE :

IN ORDER TO DRAW THIS POLLYWOG YOU USE THESE ● S · |

IN ORDER TO DRAW THIS BIRD YOU USE THESE ○ D ▲▲ · ||| ∨∨

THE DIAGRAMS ON THE FOLLOWING PAGES

WILL SHOW YOU HOW. Happy drawing, Ed Emberley

△ ○ ▭
▲ ● ▬

SHAPES

Y J L
C D S
V W M
U

LETTERS

1 2 3

NUMBERS

.   SMALL DOT

●   LARGE DOT

↓   BIRD TRACK

◎   CURLICUE

wwwww   SCRATCHY SCRIBBLE

⊙   CURLY SCRIBBLE

THINGS

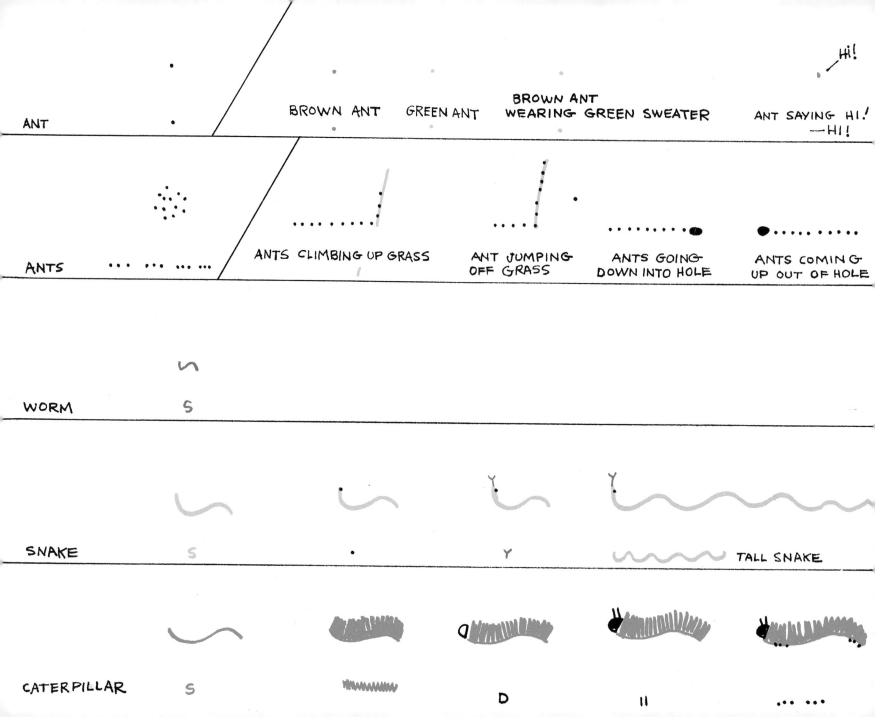

ANT

ANTS

BROWN ANT   GREEN ANT   BROWN ANT
WEARING GREEN SWEATER   ANT SAYING HI!

Hi!

—HI!

ANTS CLIMBING UP GRASS   ANT JUMPING
OFF GRASS   ANTS GOING
DOWN INTO HOLE   ANTS COMING
UP OUT OF HOLE

WORM

S

SNAKE

S   Y   TALL SNAKE

CATERPILLAR

S   D   II   ... ...

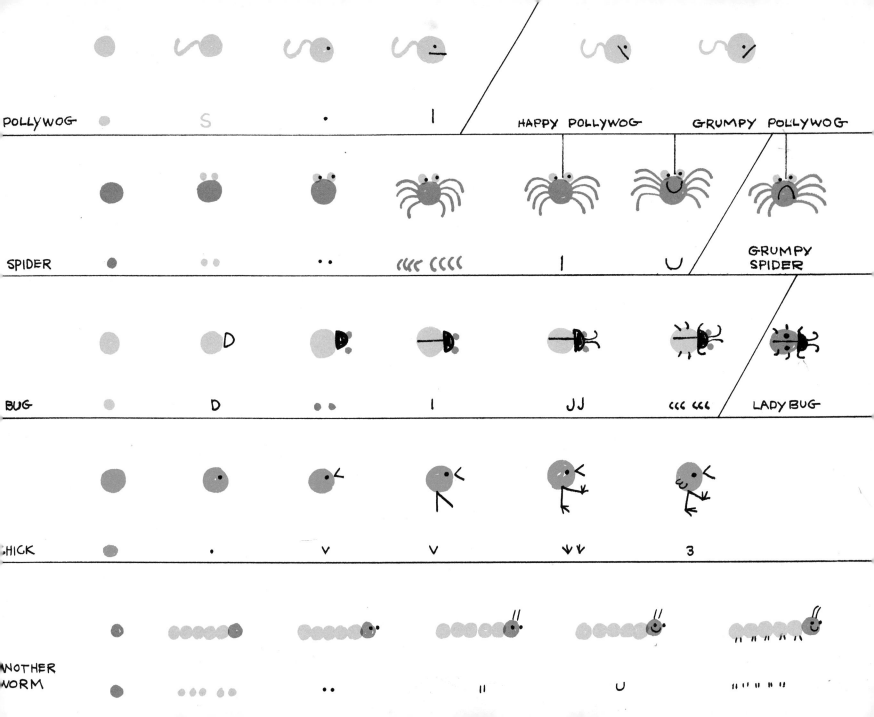

POLLYWOG   S   •   I   HAPPY POLLYWOG   GRUMPY POLLYWOG

SPIDER   •   • •   • •   ‹‹‹ ‹‹‹‹   I   U   GRUMPY SPIDER

BUG   D   • •   I   JJ   ‹‹‹ ‹‹‹   LADYBUG

CHICK   •   V   V   V V   3

MOTHER WORM   •   ••• ••   • •   II   U   ıı ıı ı ıı ı

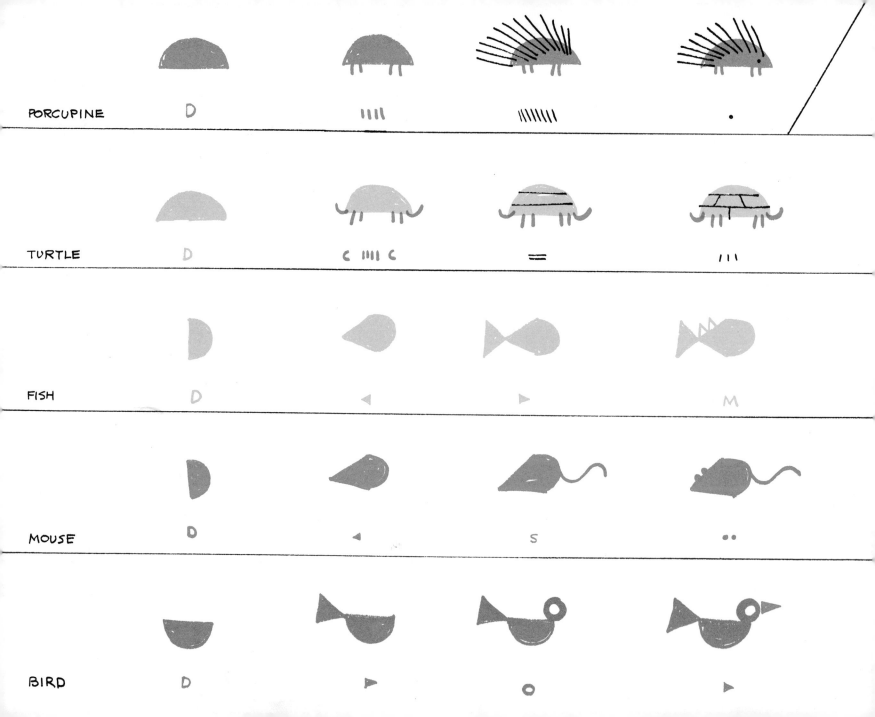

PORCUPINE

TURTLE

FISH

MOUSE

BIRD

PORCUPINE SITTING PORCUPINE SLEEPING PORCUPINE JUMPING OVER A STONE

TURTLE SLEEPING TURTLE DANCING TURTLE SKATING IN THE RAIN

.

W . | FISH SWIMMING ON HIS BACK

" " . (((||| • MOUSE, TOP VIEW

| || . ∨ ∨ 3

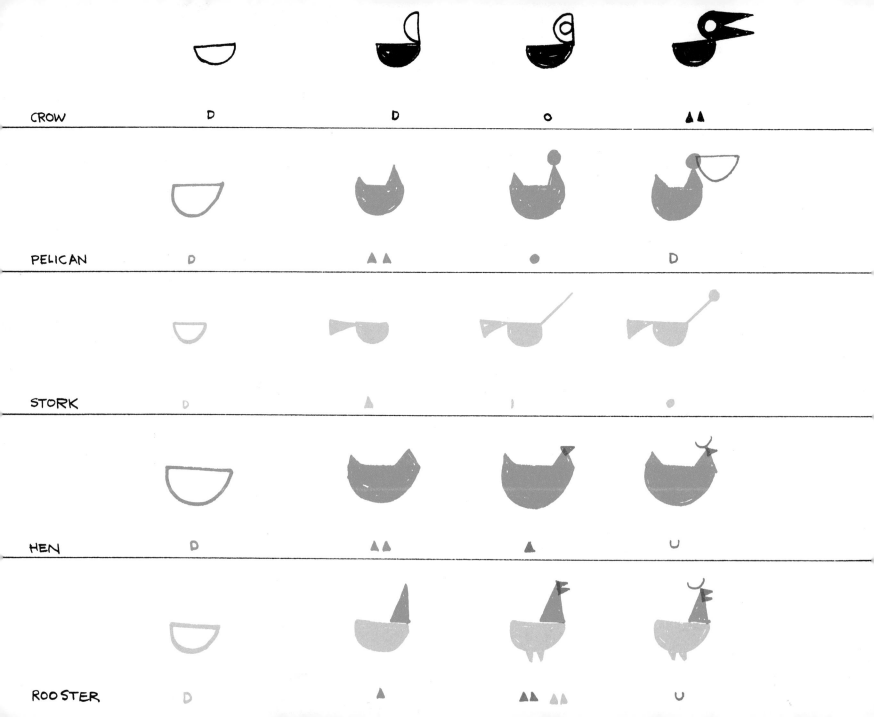

CROW

PELICAN

STORK

HEN

ROOSTER

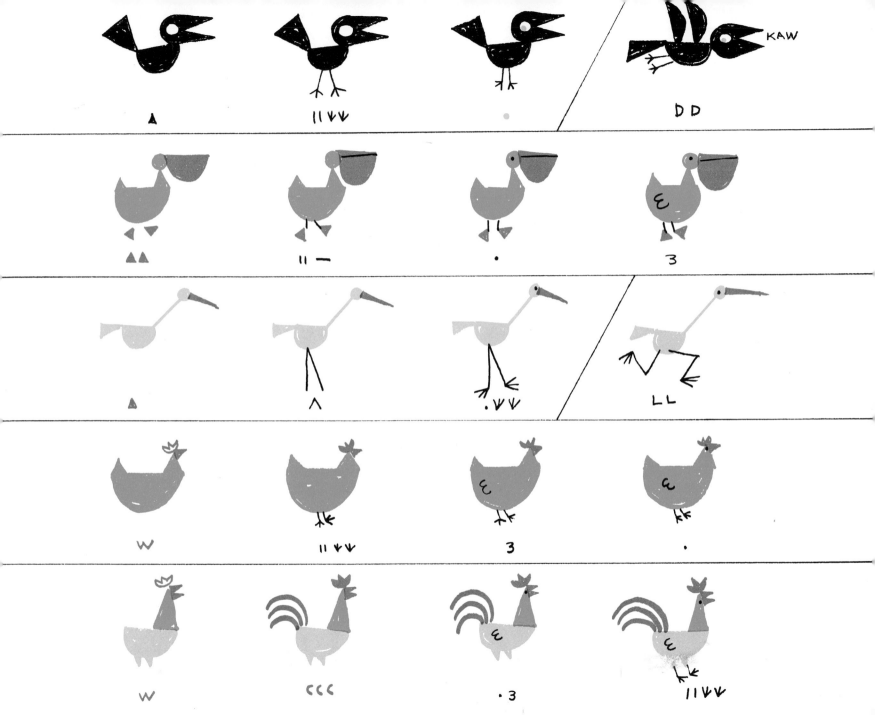

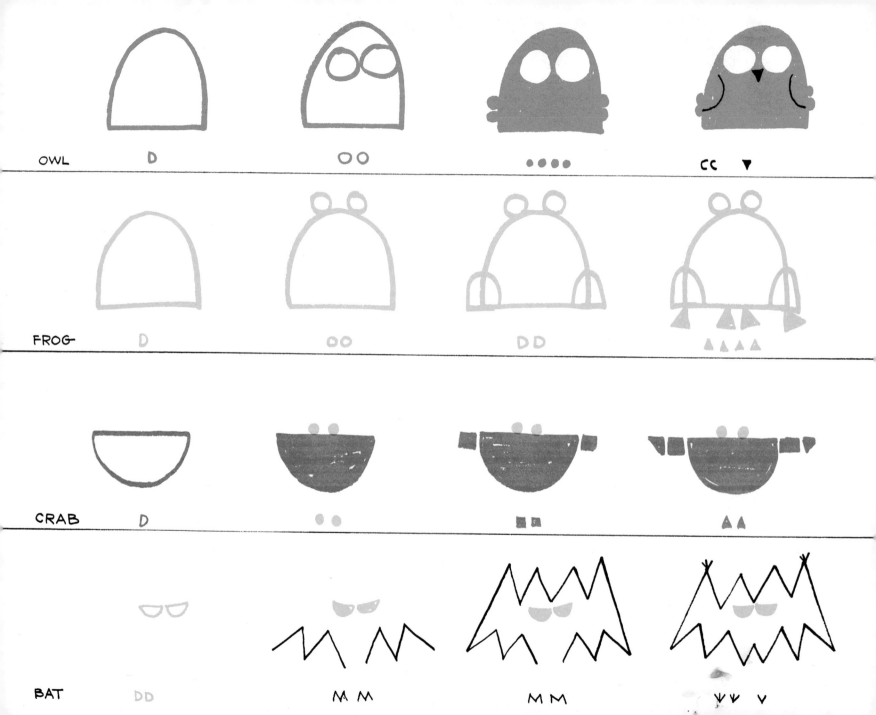

OWL   D   OO   ••••   CC ▼

FROG   D   OO   DD   ▲▲▲▲

CRAB   D   ••   ▪▪   ▲▲

BAT   DD   MM   MM   ᵥᵥ ᵥ

II ↓↓   333   D— ↓

II U   .. ••   CROAKING FROG   SLEEPING FROG

D D   ▲ ▲   (((( ))))   JJ

.. | BAT, BACK VIEW   BABY BAT

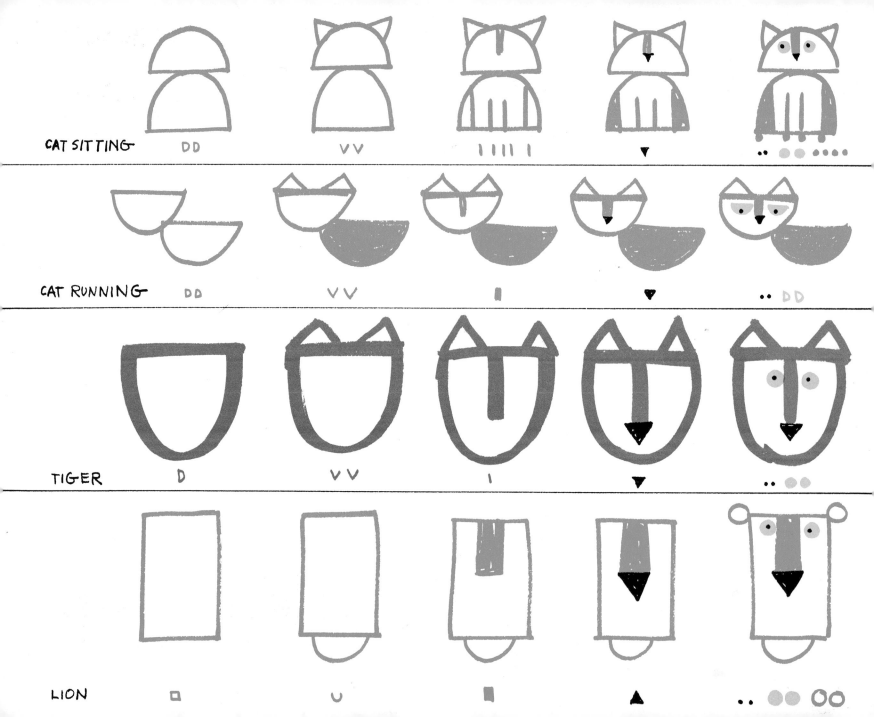

CAT SITTING   DD   VV |||||| | ▼   .. ○ ○ ○○○○

CAT RUNNING   DD   VV | ▼   .. DD

TIGER   D   VV | ▼   .. ●●

LION   □   ∪   ▮   ▲   .. ●● ○○

UU   J   III III   FAT CAT

J CCCC   ,,,, ,,, ,,, ,,, I   ,, ((((((BLACK CAT RUNNING THE OTHER WAY

Y   /// /// //   ▲▲▲▲▲▲▲▲▲▲▲

Y   VVV   ))))))))   mmm

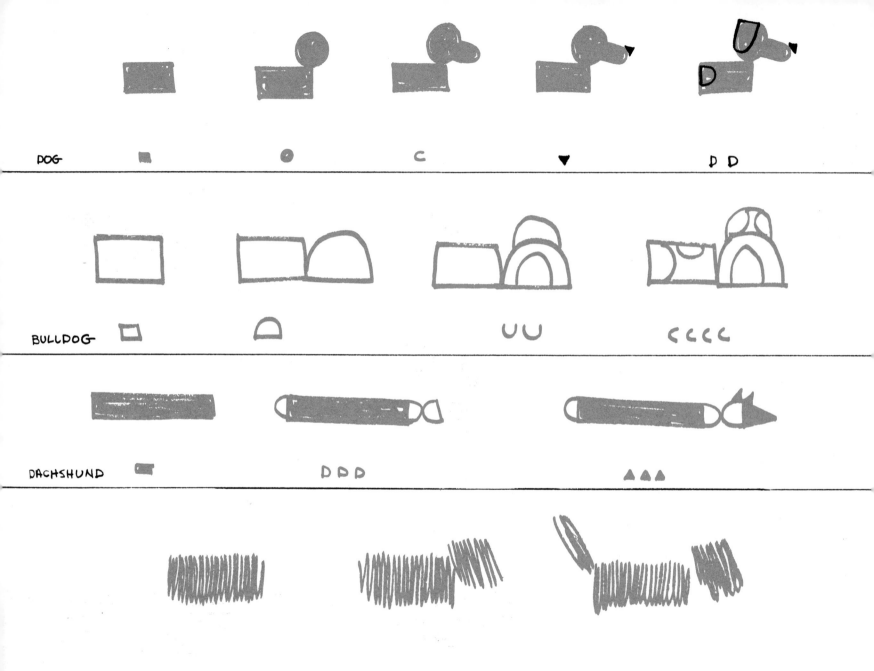

DOG

BULLDOG

DACHSHUND

SHAGGY DOG   SCRIBBLE   SCRIBBLE   SCRIBBLE

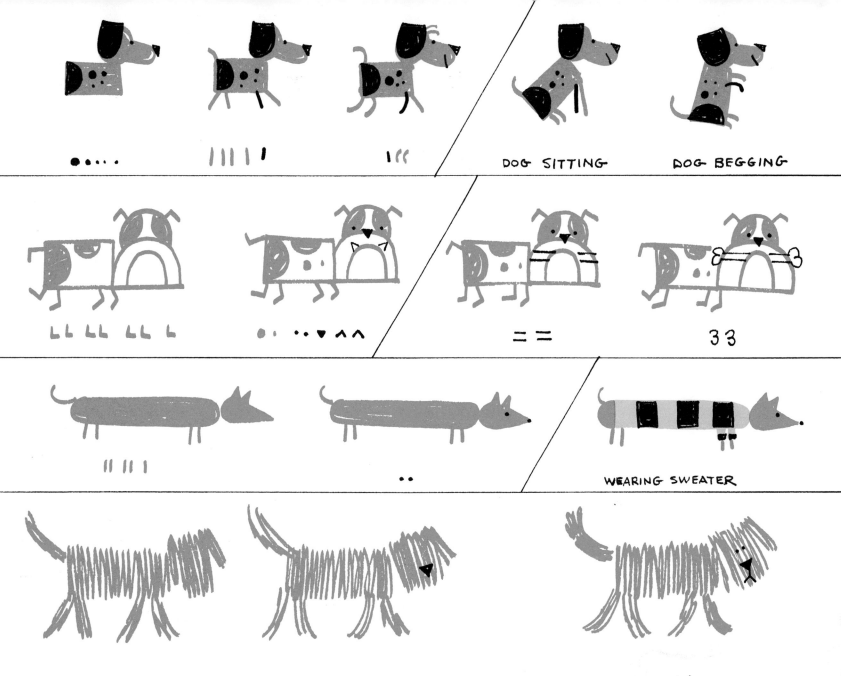

DOG SITTING   DOG BEGGING

WEARING SWEATER

SCRIBBLE

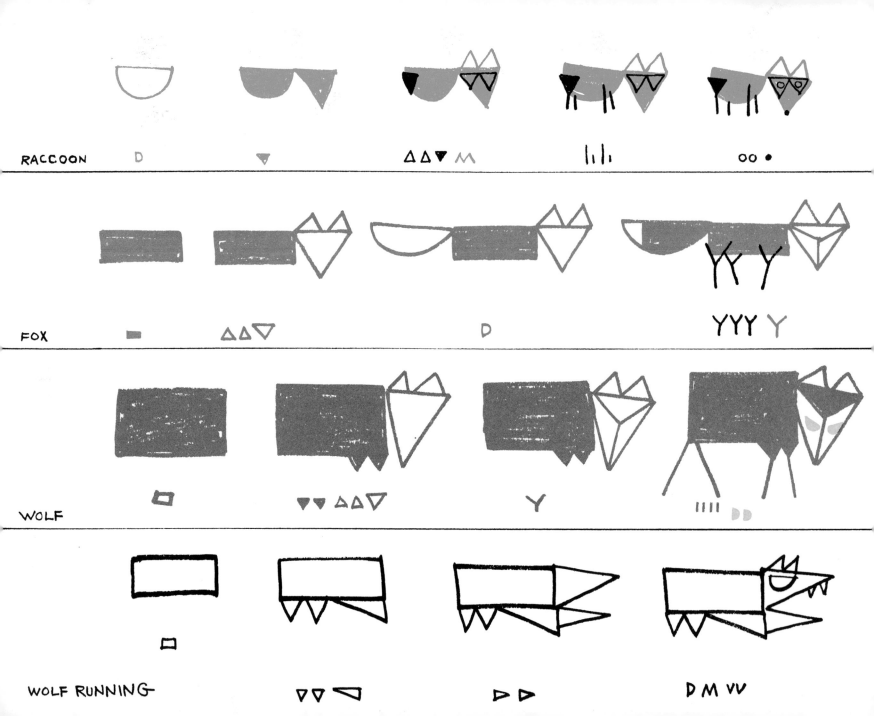

RACCOON D ▽ △△▼ ⋏ |ı|ı oo •

FOX ▬ △△▽ D YYY Y

WOLF ▱ ▼▼ △△▽ Y ||||| ᗞᗞ

WOLF RUNNING ▽▽◁ ▷▷ D M vv

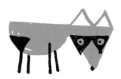

..

D

\|\|\|\|

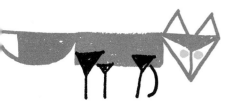
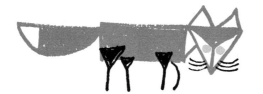

C

/ ‹‹‹ ‹‹‹

•••• •• •

••• S

S \|\|\| \|\|\| \|\|\| /// ///

WOLF LOOKING THE OTHER WAY

▲ ● \|\|\|\|\| ●

S ‹ ‹‹ ‹‹)\|\|\| •

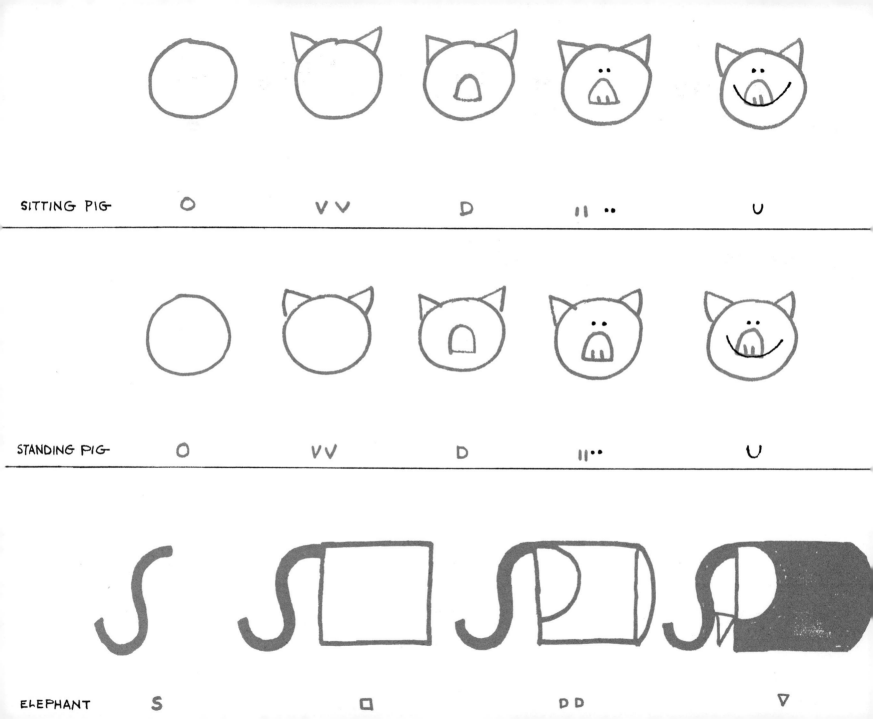

SITTING PIG   O   V V   D || ··   U

STANDING PIG   O   V V   D ||··   U

ELEPHANT   S   □   D D   ▽

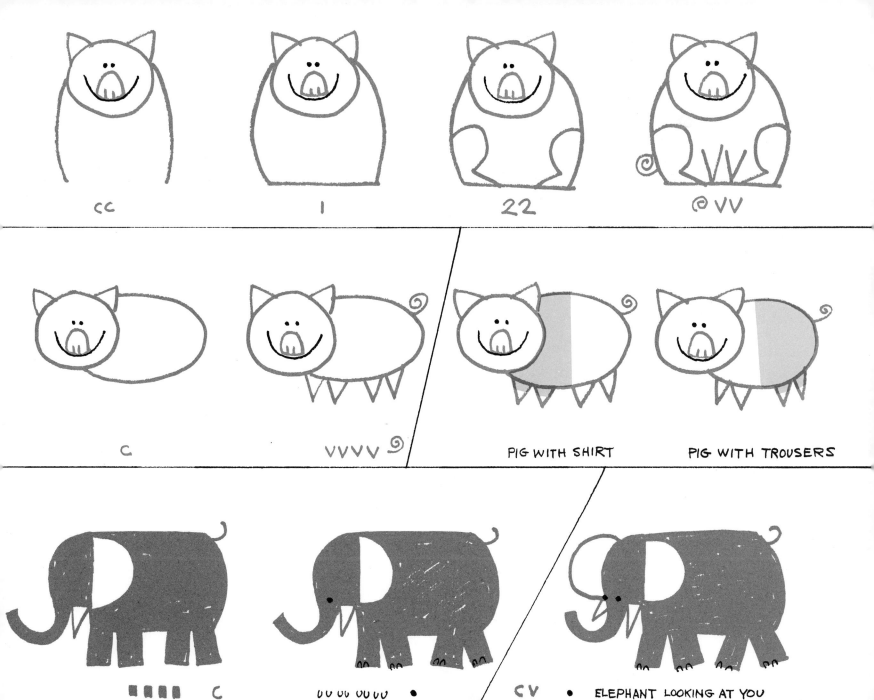

CC

I

22

@ VV

C

VVVV @

PIG WITH SHIRT

PIG WITH TROUSERS

■■■■ C

∪∪ ∪∪ ∪∪∪∪ •

CV • ELEPHANT LOOKING AT YOU

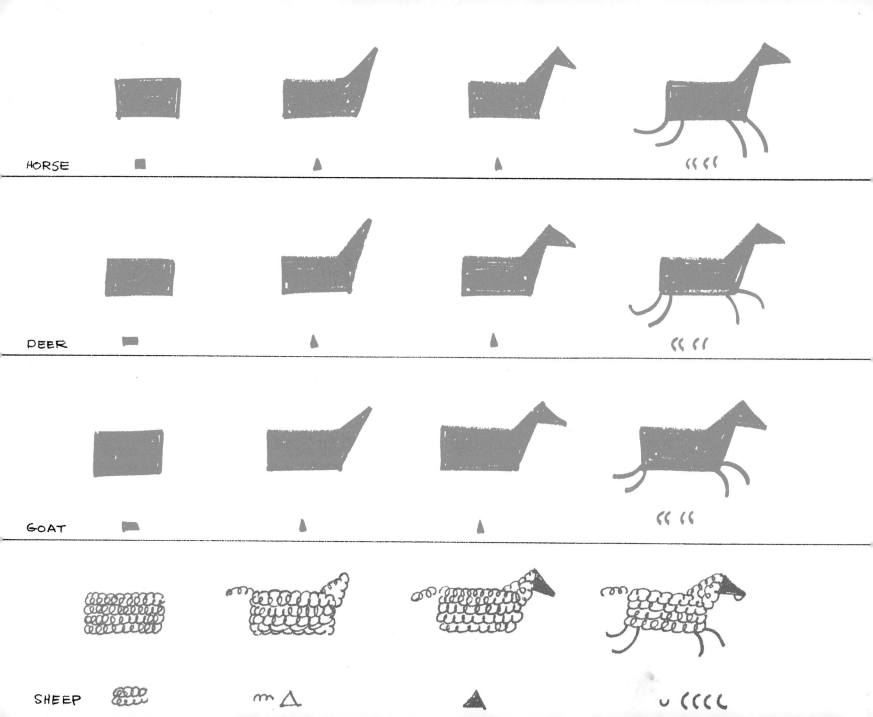

HORSE

DEER

GOAT

SHEEP

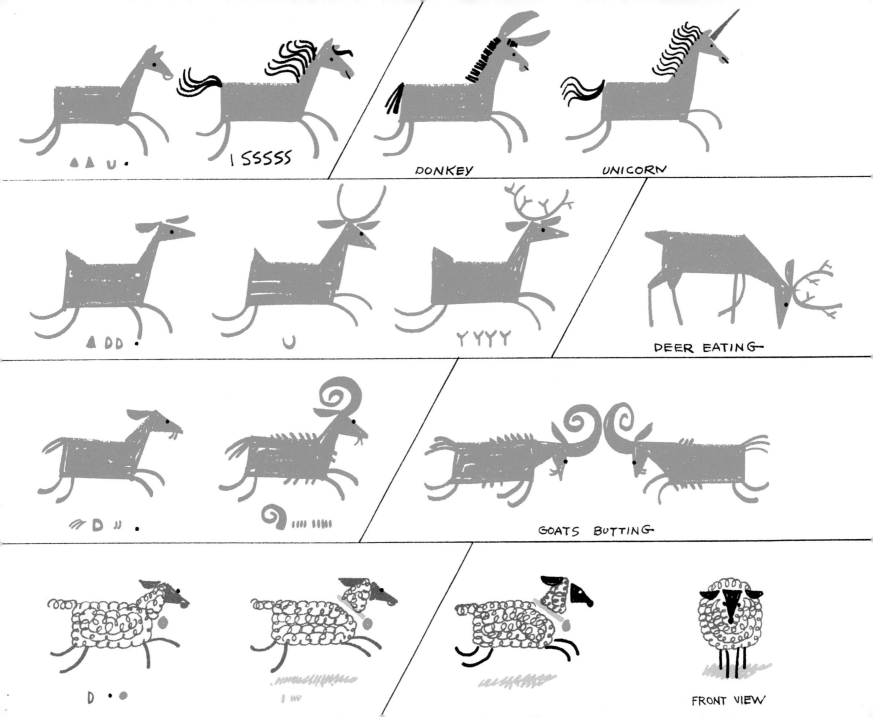

ISSSSS

DONKEY

UNICORN

DEER EATING

GOATS BUTTING

FRONT VIEW

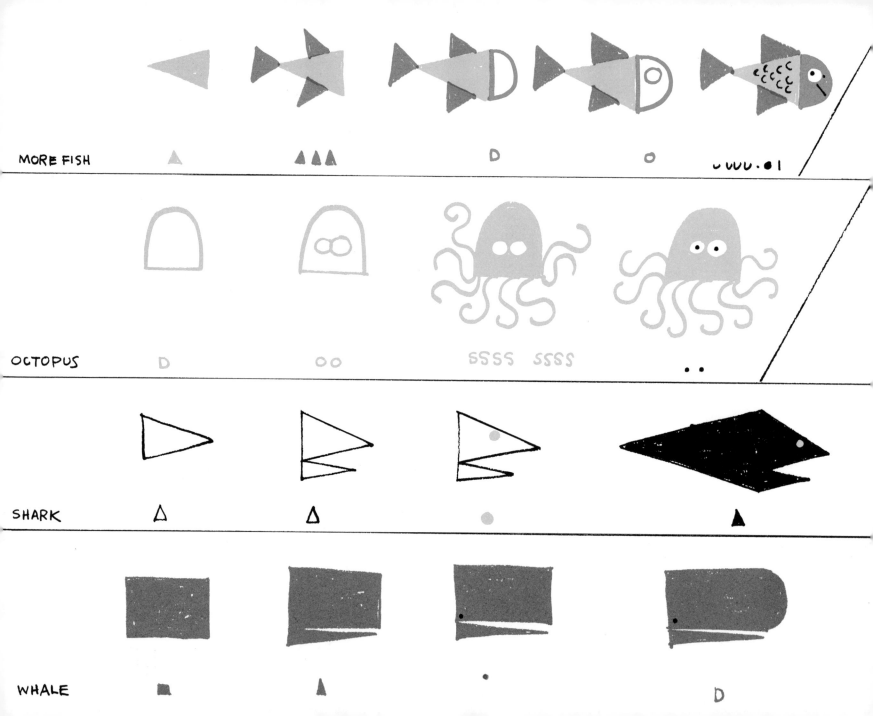

MORE FISH

OCTOPUS

SHARK

WHALE

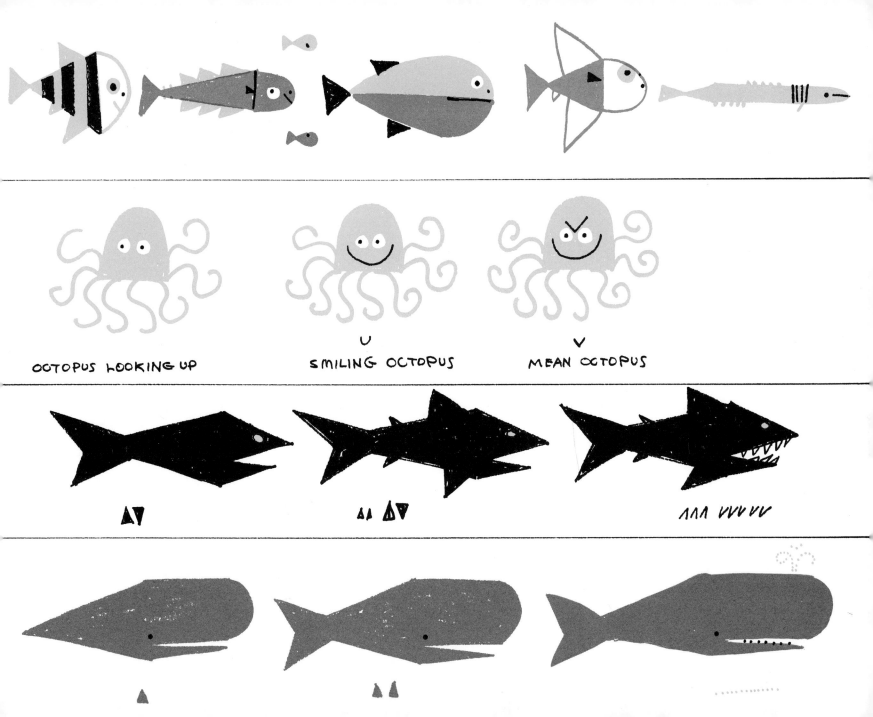

OCTOPUS LOOKING UP

SMILING OCTOPUS

MEAN OCTOPUS

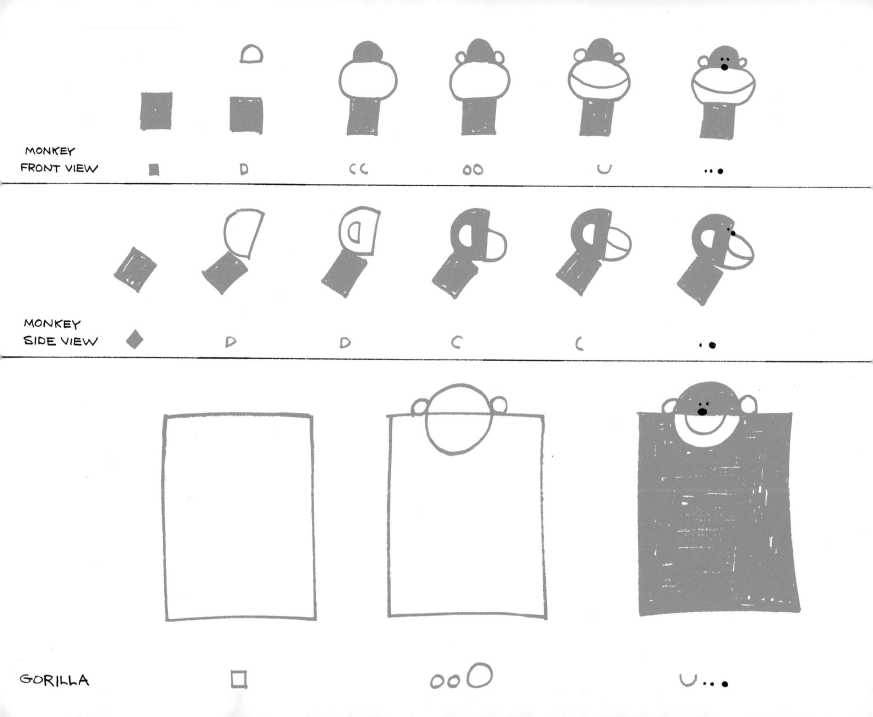

MONKEY
FRONT VIEW

MONKEY
SIDE VIEW

GORILLA

cccc

cccc

LLLL

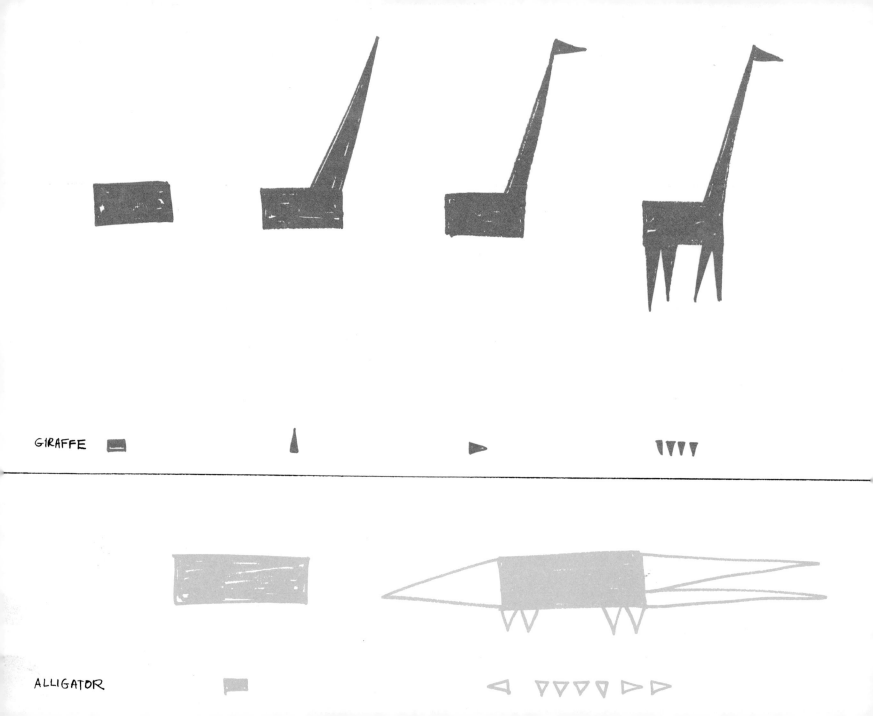

GIRAFFE

ALLIGATOR

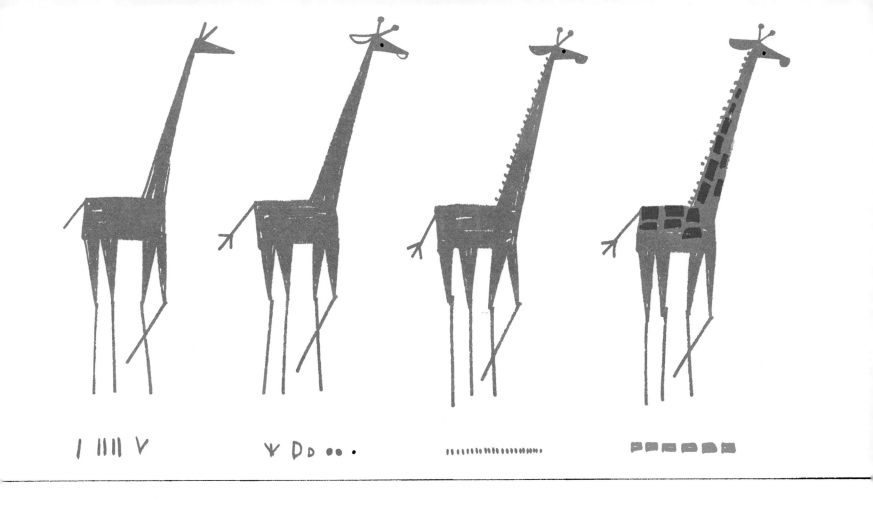

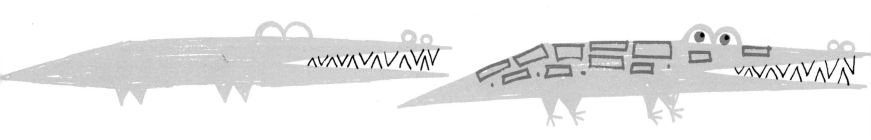

DRAGON D   SSS   SS

▲▲ VV VV I VV''''   ●● ∘∘   SS CC

/ / || || || MM V   ▲▲ ▲▲▲▲▲▲▲ ▲▲▲   ..

THERE ARE MANY WAYS YOU CAN
CHANGE THE BASIC DRAWINGS.
YOU CAN...

CHANGE COLOR

CHANGE SIZE

MAKE ONE PART LARGER

MAKE ONE PART SMALLER

DECORATE

DECORATE

PECKING

LOOKING UP

LOOKING BACK

SITTING

SINGING

RUNNING

YOU CAN MAKE PEOPLE AND ANIMALS
LOOK SAD, HAPPY, MEAN, EMBARRASSED OR
GRUMPY BY CHANGING THEIR
EYEBROWS AND/OR MOUTHS, LIKE THIS...

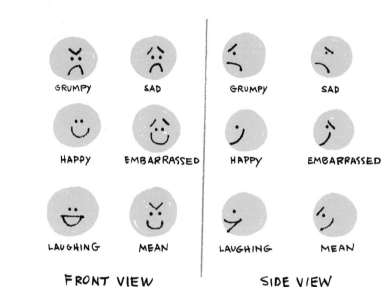

GRUMPY   SAD   GRUMPY   SAD

HAPPY   EMBARRASSED   HAPPY   EMBARRASSED

LAUGHING   MEAN   LAUGHING   MEAN

FRONT VIEW   SIDE VIEW

YOU CAN USE THIS SIMPLE METHOD OF
DRAWING TO BLOCK IN MORE COMPLICATED
DRAWINGS. FOR INSTANCE...

BLOCK IN   FILL IN   EMBELLISH